FORTNITE BATTLE ROYALE HACKS

KT-433-194

THE UNOFFICIAL GAMER'S GUIDE

FORTNITE BATTLE ROYALE HACKS

THE UNOFFICIAL GAMER'S GUIDE

TOP SECRET

BATTLE PLANS

CLASSIFIED

JASON R. RICH

STUDIO PRESS

Studio Press,
An imprint of Kings Road Publishing
Part of Bonnier Publishing
The Plaza, 535 King's Road,
London, SW10 0SZ

www.studiopressbooks.co.uk

Copyright © 2018 by Sky Pony Press

Written by Jason R. Rich
Cover designed by Brian Peterson

A CIP catalogue record for this book is available from the British Library.

Paperback ISBN: 978-1-78741-431-0
Printed in the United Kingdom
10 9 8 7 6 5 4 3 2 1

Studio Press is an imprint of Bonnier Publishing company
www.bonnierpublishing.co.uk

TABLE OF CONTENTS

SECTION 1
OVERVIEW OF FORTNIGHT: BATTLE ROYALE

You and 99 other soldiers are about to find yourselves forced off an aircraft (known as the Battle Bus). It's flying safely over a large island, but unfortunately your destiny lies on the dangerous land below.

Fortnite is really two exciting games in one. You're about to discover awesome strategies for Fortnite: Battle Royale, which has become an extremely popular game amongst PS4, Xbox One, PC, and Mac gamers.

For gamers who prefer their action on-the-go, Epic Games has released an iOS (iPhone/iPad) version of Fortnite: Battle Royale, and an Android mobile device version is expected by mid-2018. The mobile versions are compatible with the PC, Mac, PS4, and Xbox One versions of the game. As a result, you can play on your iPhone, iPad, or Android smartphone or tablet, either with or against players who are experiencing the game on other gaming systems.

© Epic Games, Inc.

You'll be forced to free fall partway to the ground, then use your Glider (parachute) to help you land safely. Your first important decision in this 100 PvP (Player Versus Player) game is to determine the best and safest place to land. As you're falling, and once you deploy the Glider, you have steering capabilities using your controller, keyboard, or touchscreen, so use them wisely.

© Epic Games, Inc.

Once you're safely on the ground and armed only with a empty backpack, a map, and a Pickaxe, it's essential that you search for and grab weapons and ammunition quickly, explore your surroundings, and gather whatever tools and resources (known as "loot") you can find. You're now smack in the middle of a survival mission. If you don't outlive all 99 of the other often heavily armed soldiers on the island, one of them will terminate you!

Only one person out of the 100 will leave the island alive. Everyone else will perish in battle or become a casualty of the deadly storm that's currently brewing.

This is no ordinary storm, however. Once it approaches the island—just minutes after your own arrival—it begins making portions of the island's land uninhabitable. In other words, if you don't avoid the storm and the areas of the island that it's taken over, first you'll find yourself getting weaker and weaker, and eventually it'll destroy you.

When the air around you turns blueish-purple, and the map displayed in the top-right corner of the screen is also covered with a purple hue, you're stuck in the deadly storm.

© Epic Games, Inc.

The ultimate goal in Battle Royale is survival, not to defeat lots of enemies. You could successfully defeat 98 adversaries, then get defeated by the 99th, which means you lose. Your goal is to become the sole survivor. There's no second place!

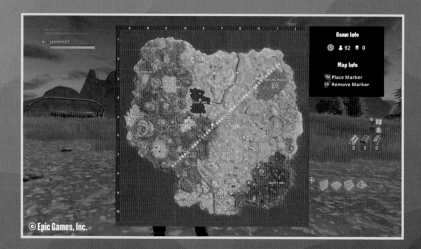

© Epic Games, Inc.

Throughout each battle, use the map to help you figure out where you are, where you need to be, and how to best avoid the deadly storm.

Use the weapons, tools, ammunition, and resources (as well as other types of loot) you discover on the island to defend yourself and defeat your enemies before they're able to annihilate you.

Fortnite: Battle Royale is no ordinary massively multiplayer, online-based shooting game. To succeed, you'll need to gather resources: wood, stone, and metal. Use the Pickaxe to smash an abandoned truck, for example, to collect metal.

© Epic Games, Inc.

Use the resources you gather from trees, rock formations, buildings, abandoned vehicles, and other objects you come across to build fortresses
and your own structures that can protect you and give you an advantage
when going on the offense against others.

Accomplishing Several Important Tasks Is Required

Welcome to Fortnite: Battle Royale, where to survive and be the last
person standing, you must simultaneously and successfully handle a
variety of tasks, including:

- Searching for and gathering resources, weapons,
  ammunition, tools, and other loot.
- Potentially fighting anyone and everyone you come into
  contact with. Defeat them before they end you. Knowing
  which weapon(s) and tools to use, and when, are key
  survival skills.
- Safely exploring pre-existing buildings, houses, structures,
  mountains, valleys, mines, junkyards, factories, forests,
  graveyards, and other terrain.

- Building your own fortresses and structures for protection, that might include traps for your enemies. Creating ramps and structures can also help you get to locations that can't easily be reached in other ways.

Do you have the speed, agility, fighting capability, resourcefulness, and intelligence to survive? This unofficial strategy guide is chock full of useful information designed to give you an edge each time you step foot on the island.

As you'll discover, even if you know exactly what to look for and what tools and weapons to use, and understand exactly where to go, nothing replaces the need for practice! To become a pro, you'll need to:

- Practice using various types of weapons.
- Perfect your building skills.
- Learn how to safely explore.
- Discover the best ways to navigate the island.

Each time you play Fortnite: Battle Royale, your experience will be different. The actions of the 99 other gamers you're competing against in real time will determine when, where, and what challenges you'll encounter, as well as the difficulty you'll have defeating each of the other soldiers. Plus, you'll need to contend with the moving storm.

Since every gamer adopts his or her own unique strategies, you'll need to adapt your own actions based on the situations you encounter and where on the island you encounter them.

Always pay attention to the terrain and how you can use your current surroundings to your advantage. Don't allow yourself to get trapped inside a building where you can't escape without being overpowered and defeated by enemies. Likewise, avoid standing for too long out in the open. Use buildings, structures, or parts of the landscape to shield yourself.

Before entering a house or building, try peeking through the windows to see if it's all clear. If not, shoot at enemies through a window, as opposed to entering the house or building first.

Don't follow roadways where snipers will be able to shoot at you from hidden locations above, or launch surprise attacks that you accidently walk, run, or tiptoe directly into.

You'll almost always have an advantage if you climb higher than your opponents, and use a mid- to long-range weapon (such as a sniper rifle or exploding projectile weapon) to defeat them. Once you get higher than your opponents, use a scoped sniper rifle or RPG, for example, to accurately target enemies below. You could also position yourself on a nearby cliff or on the roof of a pre-existing building to obtain the best views of the terrain below.

It's also possible to quickly alter the terrain by building a tower or ramp that allows you to position yourself with a bird's eye view of what's below. Here, a pathway was built between two buildings.

© Epic Games, Inc.

Various types of pistols you'll discover are great for close-range attacks, but you seldom want to get too close to opponents unless you have the element of surprise.

Always Listen Carefully

Sound plays a huge role in this game. You can hear noises created by your enemies, and they can hear sounds you make—on purpose or by accident—with your footsteps, while you're using your weapon(s), crashing through walls, gathering resources with your Pickaxe, or even opening a door, for example. In addition to using your eyes, always listen carefully!

Once you know enemies are nearby, it's important to keep track of their whereabouts so they can't launch a surprise attack at close range.

Keep in mind that running is louder than walking, especially when you're inside a building. People on higher or lower floors will hear you moving around, shooting weapons, opening Chests, or collecting loot. Likewise, if you listen carefully, you can determine the whereabouts of your enemies who are close by.

Consider using a high-quality gaming headset when playing Fortnite so you don't miss a sound. Also, when choosing your own actions, consider how much noise you'll make, especially if enemies are potentially nearby.

If you're exploring a building, for example, and you hear footsteps above or below you or on the opposite side of a doorway, and then they stop, chances are a soldier is waiting somewhere close by to attack you. Wait until you hear their footsteps moving far away before you proceed, or be prepared to battle your way out of the location you're in. Alternatively, draw a weapon and advance slowly, with extreme caution. Be ready to fight!

Instead of walking or running, which makes footstep sounds your opponents might hear, consider crouching when moving. This slows you down, but it allows you to be much quieter. Crouching when shooting a weapon also improves your aim.

Running gets you where you need to go faster, but people nearby will definitely hear you approaching.

Acquiring and Installing the Game

Fortnite is really two separate game experiences in one! One experience, Fortnite: Battle Royale, is free for all PS4, Xbox One, Windows PC, Mac gamers. All you need to do is download and install the game, and you're ready to go.

The game requires Internet connectivity, along with a membership to PlayStation Plus (PS4) or Xbox Live Gold (Xbox One). If you're a PC or Mac gamer, once you install the game, you'll connect to Epic Games's servers to experience the game. In-game purchases to unlock items and Battle Passes are optional when playing Fortnite: Battle Royale.

Several paid versions of Fortnite are also available and sold online for download, or wherever video and computer games are sold. iPhone and iPad gamers should download the free Fortnite: Battle Royal mobile app from the iOS App Store, while Android gamers will find the compatible mobile app by visiting the Google Play app store.

Shown on the Epic Games (www.epicgames.com) website (see the previous page) are Fortnite Standard Edition ($39.99), Fortnite Deluxe Edition ($59.99), Fortnight Super Deluxe Edition ($89.99), and Limited Edition ($149.99). All include Battle Royale, as well as a totally separate version of the game that includes a series of story-based "Save the World" missions.

Fortnite's Save the World missions can be experienced by one or more players simultaneously. The game version you purchase determines how many characters and how much loot comes unlocked and ready to use.

© Epic Games, Inc.

The paid editions of Fortnite (also called the "Base Game") allow you to control a broader range of characters and collect a vast assortment of exclusive loot. Your primary opponents are an army of mutant zombies.

The Save the World missions offered by the Base Game still involves fighting, exploring, and building, but the co-op PvE (Player Versus Environment / Player Versus Enemy) challenges you face will be totally different than what's offered for free when playing Battle Royale.

After installing Fortnite, one of your first tasks is to create a free Epic Games account. Provide the information that's requested.

Customize Your Gaming Experience

Seeing and hearing everything during your quest for survival in Battle Royale is essential. To fine-tune the graphics and sound you hear, as well as the control you have over your character, be sure to access the Settings menu.

To access the Settings menu, first get to this Battle Royale Lobby screen.

On the PS4, for example, press the Options button on the controller to access the gear-shaped Settings icon. On an Xbox One, PC, Mac, or your mobile device, press the appropriate button to access the Setting menu.

From the main Settings menu, toggle between the Game, Brightness, Audio, Accessibility, Input, and Wireless Controller sub-menus. The Game menu (shown here) offers a handful of player-adjustable settings related to game play.

Select Brightness, and use the Brightness Calibration option to adjust the brightness of the screen. Whether or not you actually need to make changes will depend on the lighting in the room where you're playing, as well as the monitor or screen you're using.

Access the Audio sub-menu to adjust the sound levels for Music, Sound FX, Dialogue, Voice Chat, and Cinematic. Based on the speakers or headphones you're using, consider lowering the volume of the music and boosting the volume of the Sound FX, for example, so you will hear things like footsteps and weapons fire more clearly.

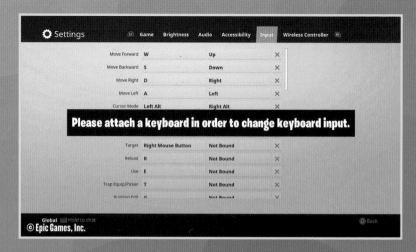

Computer gamers can customize their keyboard and mouse controls by assigning keys and buttons to handle specific tasks. This Input submenu only applies to PC and Mac gamers.

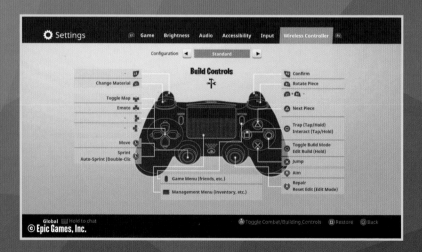

PS4 and Xbox One gamers use a wireless controller. Access the Wireless Controller submenu, and choose between the Standard (shown here), Quick Builder, and Combat Pro controller layouts.

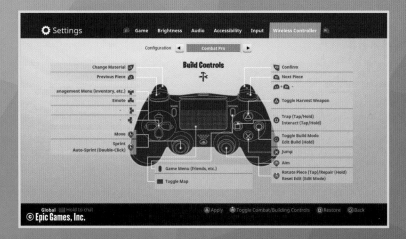

When playing Battle Royale, if your personal strategy focuses more on combat and fighting, choose the Combat Pro controller layout (shown here). However, if you use less fighting and more building as a personal strategy, use the Quick Builder layout.

Some of the controller layouts do not include the option for your soldier to crouch, for example. Instead, the focus is on making it easier to fight or quickly build within the game. The Standard controller layout is ideal for noobs and players who focus on fighting, building, and exploring as their primary strategy.

Choose a Game Play Mode

Battle Royale has several game modes: Solo, Duo, Squad, and Solid Gold. Choose which mode you want to experience from the Lobby screen. Press the appropriate button on your controller (or keyboard) to select the Change Mode option.

Choose a game play mode from the Change Mode menu. Solo mode allows you to compete against 99 other adversaries. Duo mode (shown near the bottom-right corner of the screen) allows you to team up with one friend. Your goal is to defeat all 98 other enemies.

In Squad mode, gather a group of friends who will fight together as a team against everyone else.

In Solid Gold mode, all Supply Drops contain Legendary weapons, which are the rarest and most powerful weapons. You can play alone, or create a team of two, three, or four players. After Solid Gold mode is selected, select one of the player positions located to the right and left of your character to add a second, third, or fourth player to your team. The friend(s) you want to add to your team must already be an online Friend, and they must be logged into the game.

SECTION 2
CHOOSING AND CUSTOMIZING YOUR HERO

As of March 2018, Epic Games considered Fortnite: Battle Royale to still be in a "Early Access" development phase, meaning the game was not 100 percent completed. Changes and updates are regularly being made.

While everyone has full access to the game, new weapons, characters, and game play elements, as well as alterations to the island map, are continuously being added or tweaked.

Gamers who've purchased the Base Game can choose their character for the Save the World missions. So far, however, Epic Games has not added the ability to switch soldiers when playing Battle Royale. (This is expected to change in the future.) As of March 2018, the hero you'll be controlling is randomly assigned to you the very first time you play.

From the Lobby, it's possible to customize your hero's appearance by earning or purchasing loot. Specific items are sold within the Item Shop (shown on the previous page.)

To make in-game purchases, you'll first need to visit the Store (also from the Lobby), then use real money to acquire V-Bucks. These V-Bucks can then be redeemed for Battle Passes or specific items.

All items available from the Item Shop allow you to alter the appearance of your character, but these items *do not* impact a soldier's abilities within the game. Items offered within the Shop change daily. Link the Items you acquire with your character from the Locker (shown here), which is also accessible from the Lobby.

HACKS FOR FORTNITE

© Epic Games, Inc.

If you've purchased or acquired the Sawtooth, you can link it with your character and it will replace the standard Pickaxe.

© Epic Games, Inc.

By purchasing Battle Passes, or acquiring free Battle Passes, it's possible to unlock exclusive or limited-edition loot and items that allow you to customize your soldier's appearance and actions.

© Epic Games, Inc.

Battle Passes encourage you to reach specific goals during battles. Each time an objective is achieved, new loot and items get unlocked.

Once you've acquired more than one outfit (skin) for your character, switch between them from the Locker to dramatically alter their appearance. Shown here is the default Blue Team Leader outfit.

This is the Mission Specialist outfit for the same character. As you can see, she looks totally different.

The Sub Commander outfit looks particularly intimidating, especially if you add the Backup Plan Back Bling, for example.

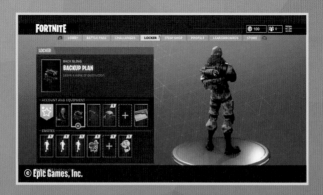

Also from the Locker, once you collect the appropriate items, you're able to add optional Back Bling to your soldier to enhance how they look from behind. Remember, no matter how badass your soldier looks, the items you add to enhance his or her appearance don't improve their strength or capabilities during a battle.

Occasionally free Battle Passes are offered through special promotions, which you can learn about from Epic Games's website (www.epicgames. com). For example, if you're an Amazon Prime member and have a Twitch. tv account, free Battle Passes are periodically offered.

© Epic Games, Inc.

Regardless of which hero you're controlling, during each battle two things must be maintained to ensure your soldier's continued survival: Health and Shields. The meters for Health and Shields are always displayed near the bottom-center of the screen during battles.

Displayed in the bottom-center of the screen is your Shield and Health meter. Your Health meter starts at 100HP, while your Shield meter starts at 0HP. As you take damage from incoming attacks, for example, first your Shields (if you have them) get depleted. Then your Health begins to diminish. Using potions and special drinks, it's possible to boost your Shields up to 200HP.

When both the Health and Shield meters reach zero, your time in the battle comes to an immediate end. However, using items (loot) you collect, it's often possible to replenish your Health and/or Shields during a battle so you can stay alive longer.

Keep in mind that Shields do not protect your soldier from falls, so avoid accidently falling off buildings or cliffs. It is often possible, however, to slide down steep cliffs safely.

SECTION 3
SURVIVAL IS ALWAYS YOUR MAIN OBJECTIVE

Most gamers adopt one of three main strategies when playing Battle Royale. They either focus mainly on combat, survival and building, or on all three of these activities.

© Epic Games, Inc.

Choosing a primarily combat strategy requires you to begin gathering the best weapons and survival gear—such as Medical Packs, Shield Potions, and Bandages—starting the moment you land on the island. Then you systematically seek out enemies, launch attacks, and defeat as many as you can, as fast as you can.

The combat strategy approach requires practice working with many of the different weapons you find, plus discovering the best ways to approach, surprise, and attack opponents without receiving too much damage yourself. Some weapons are easier to aim than others, and some offer better accuracy or unlimited ammo.

The more practice you have working with many different types of weapons, the better off you'll be in battle. You can't always decide which weapons you'll be carrying. You often have to grab whatever weapon(s), items, and ammo you manage to find.

© Epic Games, Inc.

Using a survival strategy also requires you to gather weapons, but instead of running around fighting early on, stay clear of enemies. While taking time to explore, gather resources and loot that'll come in handy later. Wait until late in the battle, when far fewer enemies are still alive (and the inhabitable part of the island is much smaller), before you're forced to engage in combat.

© Epic Games, Inc.

If you're hiding, be sure to have a weapon in hand, and continuously be on the lookout for approaching enemies. When in close range, whichever fighter spots the other first is typically the one who shoots first and wins. Notice the ammo box on the shelf (on the right side of the screen, shown on the previous page.) When you come across one of these, open it to stock up on ammo.

© Epic Games, Inc.

You don't necessarily need to build a structure to hide in, although doing this offers greater protection from enemy fire. When appropriate, you can simply crouch and hide in a bush, for example. This offers no protection other than making you harder to spot, but it could give you the element of surprise as an enemy approaches.

In some Chests and Supply Drops, you can find camouflage bushes, and use them to disguise yourself and be able to move around with this camouflage around you. However, if you take any damage, the bush camouflage disappears. Be sure to crouch when using a bush as camouflage so you stay as hidden as possible. If you see a moving bush, you know someone is hiding in it, so attack it with a mid- to long-range weapon or an explosive such as a grenade.

© Epic Games, Inc.

To succeed using the survival and building approach, you'll need to: 1. Master your building skills. 2. Discover the best places and ways to hide. 3. Make sure you're prepared to finish off the final enemies at the end of the battle with the most powerful projectile, explosive, and long-range weapons you've gathered.

A third option is to combine combat and survival strategies throughout each battle. To be successful, you'll need plenty of practice to master all of your gaming skills. Remember, the key to success in Fortnite: Battle Royal is to try to be the last person standing. The number of enemies you defeat is far less important.

You're also rewarded for how long you stay alive during a battle, and the number of Chests you find and open, as well as which locations of the map you visit, for example.

© Epic Games, Inc.

Almost all Chests include at least one powerful weapon, ammo, and a Shield Potion or Bandages. As long as it's safe to do so, Chests are always worth opening.

© Epic Games, Inc.

When you open a Chest, its contents spread out around you. Figure out what's worth grabbing, and if necessary, re-organize your inventory (backpack) to accommodate the new weapons and loot. You may need to give up something you already have and replace it with something better or more powerful. If you need extra time to sort through a Chest's contents, first build walls around you and the loot for protection.

Choosing the Best Landing Location

From the Lobby, select the Play option for Battle Royale mode. You will be transported to the pre-deployment area.

© Epic Games, Inc.

While wandering around the pre-deployment area, look around for weapons and practice your shooting skills. Unfortunately, once you board the Battle Bus, whatever weapons you find will be left behind. You can not harm anyone or be harmed in the pre-deployment area. Each battle actually kicks off once you jump out of the Battle Bus.

From the moment the Battle Bus approaches the island, you have just over 30 seconds to determine the best time to jump out and start falling toward the ground. If you wait too long, you'll automatically be ejected from the bus before it fully passes over the island.

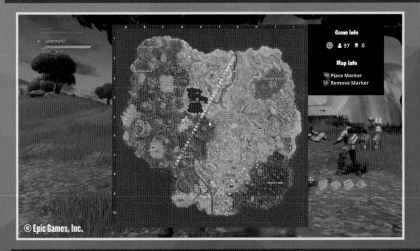

The Battle Bus always approaches the island from a different direction. Access this map to see from where you'll be approaching before you jump out. You can do this while in the pre-deployment area only. The yellow line through the map shows the flight path the Battle Bus will take.

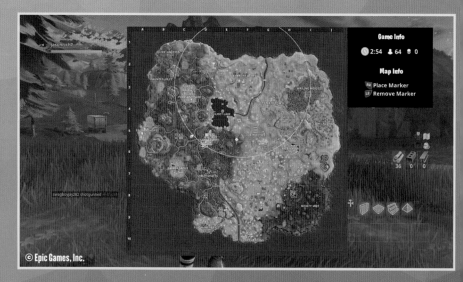

© Epic Games, Inc.

Many areas of the map have names. These are considered "Points of Interest." Each location offers different terrain, pre-existing structures, and a different selection of Chests, weapons, ammo, tools, and resources. You can access this map anytime once you land on the island.

© Epic Games, Inc.

© Epic Games, Inc.

When and where you leave the Battle Bus determines where you'll be able to land. After ejecting from the bus, you'll be in a free fall and headed downwards toward the island below.

From the free fall position, use the controller to position yourself into a nosedive. This allows you to reach the ground much faster and gives you more control over your direction, so you can approach a desired landing area more precisely.

© Epic Games, Inc.

To avoid landing with a life-finishing splat, you're given a Glider (parachute). During your fall, choose to deploy (open) it at anytime. If you wait too long, the Glider will open automatically. With the Glider active, you fall much slower, and have precise navigational control over where you'll land.

As you're falling, it's possible to switch between free fall and using the Glider several times before you reach the ground. Figure out what works best in order to navigate to your desired landing spot.

Depending on how you plan to approach the battle, you can opt to land in an area that's filled with buildings and structures, or target your landing to a more secluded spot. The sooner you leave the Battle Bus, and the faster you nosedive toward land, the better your chances are of beating your enemies to the ground and finding the available weapons in your landing area before someone else does.

As you're free falling, if you see adversaries attempting to land near where you planned to land, but they're closer to the ground than you or they've already landed, consider choosing an alternate landing spot. Immediately upon landing, find cover and evaluate your surroundings, or start grabbing weapons you spot nearby.

Inside buildings is where you'll likely find weapons, ammo, bombs, first-aid items, traps, and tools, as well as Chests that can be opened to reveal more useful loot. If you look carefully as you're falling from the Battle Bus after you've activated your Glider, you can often spot the glow of Chests and available weapons from above. The glow from weapons and Chests you'll see offer clues about the best places to land. Look on roofs and inside windows as you're falling for objects that are glowing.

Instead of landing on the ground near buildings or structures and then having to approach them and climb up or down stairs, or build a ramp, for example, try landing on a structure's roof or an open platform on a higher floor. This will save you time once you land and potentially help you find and grab weapons and ammo faster.

The popular areas of the island that have the most Chests, weapons, ammo, and other loot to gather tend to be where your opponents will opt to land as well. Thus, if you arrive after others, you'll discover empty Chests instead of full ones.

If you're not one of the first people to land on the ground and reach the places where items are located, you can easily find yourself landing, then being defeated almost instantly by someone who grabbed a gun or weapon first, and simply waited for your late arrival.

Landing in less popular and more secluded areas means you'll sometimes find fewer weapons and items, but you'll encounter many more trees and stones. Use the Pickaxe to gather these two essential resources.

It's near buildings and on roads, for example, that you'll typically find abandoned cars, trucks, buses, and other metal objects. Use your Pick-axe on these items to gather metal. When it comes to building structures, metal allows you to create walls, floors, and ceilings, for example, that can withstand the most damage before collapsing.

Since you can choose which material you build with, use brick or metal for walls that need to withstand enemy attacks, and use wood to create ramps, bridges, or stairs, unless you'll be using them for protection, as opposed to climbing.

© Epic Games, Inc.

Certain areas of the island, such as Pleasant Park, Retail Row, Loot Lake, and Anarchy Acers, are known to be heavily populated with the strongest weapons and items, along with the most Chests. Reach these areas first to gather the best selection of things you'll ultimately need to survive. Shown here is a lovely view of Loot Lake from the outskirts.

If you miss out on grabbing powerful weapons or extra ammo, for example, when you defeat an opponent, everything they previously gathered and stored in their backpack becomes yours to take. Defeating a well-stocked enemy is a great way to improve your personal arsenal.

After defeating an enemy from mid- to long range, don't immediately run up to the items the enemy has left behind. Move forward with caution, and watch out for other adversaries who saw your conquest and are now waiting to shoot at you as soon as you attempt to grab the abandoned loot. Keep a close eye on your surroundings as you approach, build protective walls and barriers if necessary, and be ready for surprise attacks from snipers located above you.

© Epic Games, Inc.

The very first thing to do once you land on the island is to locate and grab at least one weapon, preferably a mid- to long-range gun, along with some ammo. A Rocket Launcher, for example, will defeat any enemy from a distance, plus destroy a structure someone is hiding in.

© Epic Games, Inc.

Once you've gathered multiple items, including several weapons, be sure to access your backpack inventory and organize what's in there so you can access the most frequently used items and weapons the fastest. Taking even a few seconds to scroll through items, to locate a weapon you need when an enemy is right in front of you could put you at a huge disadvantage. The result will be your untimely defeat. Wasting valuable time during a battle can be dangerous.

What You Should Know About the Island Map

As less and less of the island stays habitable due to the storm, you and your adversaries will be forced to keep moving until you either get defeated or you become one of the few remaining soldiers in the storm's small inner circle, where the final battles ensue.

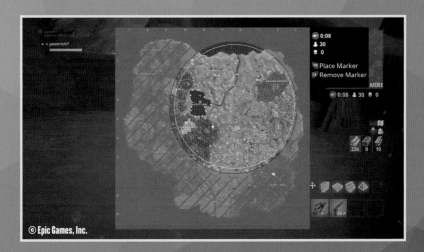

© Epic Games, Inc.

When looking at the map during a battle, it's possible to quickly determine where important points of interest can be found and what parts of the island are uninhabitable due to the storm (the purple area).

By looking at the map, it's also possible to quickly calculate approximately how long it'll take you to get from one location to another. The map is divided into a grid. When the terrain is flat, each square of the grid takes approximately 45 seconds for most of the soldiers to travel across. It takes longer if it's necessary to climb hills or over obstacles.

© Epic Games, Inc.

The location of loot and weapons is randomized for each battle. However, the location of each Chest is always the same. So once you discover where Chests are located, anytime you return to that location in later battles, you'll find Chests in the same exact locations. What they contain may be different, however.

Anytime Epic Games releases a game update, you may discover additional Chests in various locations, or discover that new points of interest have been added to the island. For example, in the February 28, 2018 game update, a new point of interest, called Lucky Landing, was added to the southern edge of the island.

Discover Points of Interest on the Island

You can always look at a detailed map during a battle. However, the following chart will help you choose the best landing spots and let you know what to expect in each area of the island.

Each location offers loot and Chests. The more stars the Amount of Loot column of this chart contains, the more plentiful the loot and the higher the number of Chests will be. Keep in mind that Epic Games periodically adds new points of interest to the map, plus tweaks of what can be found and collected in each location, so expect to encounter additional locations on the island as time goes on.

POINT OF INTEREST NAME	AMOUNT OF LOOT	DESCRIPTION
Anarchy Acres	***	Located in the North. Look for large barns and silos, which contain lots of loot. At the same time, avoid spending too much time in the open fields, because you'll be easy to spot. Use the Pickaxe on the tractors to collect metal.
Dusty Depot	*	Located near the center of the map, this region contains several large warehouse buildings. In these warehouses, however, is only a small selection of weapons and loot, and few Chests, so it may not be worth your time or the risk to visit, unless you're forced to by the storm.
Fatal Fields	****	Located in the South. This area has a bunch of large barns that contain plenty of loot and Chests. There are also a bunch of nearby hills where you can hide, if necessary. From the top of a hill, it's possible to look down and shoot at enemies.
Flush Factory	***	Located in the South, this location offers less loot and is a good distance from the center of the map. It's a toilet factory, so be sure to check the bathroom—without getting flushed by your adversaries.
Greasy Grove	*****	This is one of the map's more popular locations because there's a ton of loot to be collected. It's located in the Southwestern area of the map, and features fast food restaurants, a gas station, and other businesses and homes to explore. Stock up on metal in and around these buildings. Expect to encounter a lot of other enemy soldiers here, so be prepared for fights.

(Continued on next page)

Haunted Hills	***	Located near the Northwest corner of the map, this dark and gloomy area has old churches and gravestones, as well as creepy crypts to explore. As always, check each building carefully for loot and Chests. You'll find great stuff inside many of the stone crypts that surround the church.
Junk Junction	*	Located in the Northwest portion of the island, this junkyard offers a great place to collect metal and explore, but there's not too much loot to be found. You'll be better off if you already have a few weapons before entering this area, in case you encounter enemies.
Lonely Lodge	***	Located in the East, this area contains a lot of woods, a few smaller huts, and a RV camp. If you climb to the top of the watchtower, you'll see a great distance in all directions. This tends to be a less popular landing location.
Loot Lake	***	What sets this point of interest apart is the huge lake. You'll need plenty of wood to build platforms, ramps, and bridges in order to navigate around.
Lucky Landing	*****	There is a ton of loot and multiple Chests to be discovered in this Asian-inspired region. Lucky Landing is located along the south coast of the island. It's very easy to spot from the Battle Bus because many of the buildings have bright red roofs. There's also a giant pink tree in the center of one building.

Moisty Mire	*****	Located in the Southeast potion of the island, this is a swampy area filled with log cabins. Be sure to check inside the cabins, as well as in hollowed-out trees, for loot. Collect plenty of extra wood here, because you'll need to build platforms and ramps to travel around easily, especially in the swamp. In the nearby prison, be sure to search the cells and guard towers carefully for loot.
Pleasant Park	*****	Located in the Northwest area of the map, many small- to mid-size buildings populate this region. Instead of entering the front door of buildings, it's often easier to climb up to the roof (from the outside using a ramp you build), then use the Pickaxe to smash your way downwards into the attic or top floor. This is a good area to stock up on metal.
Retail Row	*****	Located to the west of Lonely Lodge, this is one of the most popular points of interest on the map. There are a ton of buildings to explore, and most are chock full of loot. Plan on encountering of a lot of enemies in this region. Fighting will likely be required almost immediately upon landing (or reaching this location). If you plan to take a combat approach to your gaming strategy, this is a great place to land.
Salty Springs	*****	Located in the Southern area of the map, this is a popular point of interest that contains a lot of loot and multiple Chests. You need to be one of the first to arrive in order to get the best selection, or you'll wind up having to fight aggressively in order to build up your inventory and survive your visit here.

(Continued on next page)

Shifty Shafts	*	This area contains an old mine, so plan on exploring a maze of underground tunnels. Have a weapon in hand as you explore, because you don't know who will be waiting around each bend.
Snobby Shores	*****	Welcome to the suburbs (located in the West). Here, you'll find large homes in what was once an upscale neighborhood. There is a lot of loot and multiple Chests to be found here, but you'll need to search each home carefully. If you find a home's basement or attic, chances are that's where the best loot and Chests can be found.
Tilted Towers	*****	Located in the Southern region of the map, this is a popular place to land, so plan on encountering a bunch of enemies right away. If you have time, explore each building in this region.
Tomato Town	*	This is a rather remote location with not much loot. If you wind up here, however, be sure to smash the walls of the bridge to discover some hidden loot.
Wailing Woods	*	Here in this secluded and rather large forest (located in the Northeast portion of the map), you'll find plenty of trees. Collect wood while you're here, but when the storm comes, be far away because it'll take you a long time to get out of the woods, and the storm will often deplete your Health before you can escape.

Here's what Anarchy Acres looks like.

Check out this view of Greasy Grove.

Greasy Grove offers many buildings to explore, including fast food restaurants and gas stations.

This is what it looks like from the outskirts of Retail Row.

Inside the shops and restaurants there's lots of metal to be collected. Search around for some useful loot and weapons as well. Just don't get yourself shot through a window by someone lurking outside.

Snobby Shores is where you'll find lovely mansions. Inside them are Chests, weapons, and other loot that's worth grabbing.

Haunted Hills contains a bunch of stone crypts surrounding the church that often contain goodies, so check inside each of them carefully.

Here's an overview of the Flush Factory region. Explore each building separately.

The buildings in Flush Factory are massive. Start from the ground floors of each and work your way to higher levels, or climb to a roof, smash your way in through the roof using the Pickaxe, and work your way from the higher levels downwards. Either way, you'll discover lots of loot. Be prepared to encounter enemy soldiers as well.

The red roofs of Lucky Landing can be seen as you disembark the Battle Bus. Keep an eye out for the large pink tree as well.

The massive pink tree in Lucky Landing is right in the center of the area, sticking out of a building. If you enter the building and use your Pickaxe, this tree is an excellent source of wood.

Island Exploration Strategies

Depending on where you are on the island, the type of terrain that surrounds you, the location of the storm, where your opponents might be hiding, and where you need to get to, choose a strategy for traveling around the island that will keep you safe.

When forced to move, avoid staying out in the open. Following a road or clearly labeled path, for example, is seldom a smart move. You're easy to spot and snipers can typically shoot at you from overhead. Run, don't walk, through open areas.

Try to stay hidden or well protected by nearby surroundings (trees, rock formations, pre-existing structures, buildings, abandoned trucks, and structures you build) as you move around.

Sometimes you'll be forced to move forward without cover. In this situation, run in a zigzag formation and jump a lot, so you're not an easy target. Avoid moving in a straight line or following a predictable path whenever you're out in the open and vulnerable to attack.

Hide behind trees or collect wood here in Wailing Woods. Create a ramp/stairs, and you can climb to the top of a tree to see what's around you.

© Epic Games, Inc.

Especially in areas that have a lot of pre-built buildings and structures, you'll often find piles of tires. While these can't be collected and used as a building resource, you can jump on them and use them as a trampoline in order to quickly reach a higher level of a nearby building or structure, for example.

© Epic Games, Inc.

Any time you enter into houses or buildings, you'll be required to open doors. By default, a door is closed unless you or someone else has opened it. To help cover your tracks, close doors after opening and proceeding through them. If you leave a door open, this offers a clue to your adversaries that you might be inside, or that the location has already been explored.

If you discover a new weapon and want to test it out, don't! That is, unless you know you're alone in a secluded area. The noise from the weapon could attract enemies to your location or reveal where you are.

As you explore the island, try to stay on high ground as much as possible. This means climbing along the tops of hills, mountains, cliffs, or buildings. The higher you are, the more terrain you can see. Plus, it's easier to spot and shoot at enemies if you're above them shooting downwards.

Create tall towers, bridges, and elevated pathways between pre-existing structures (shown here) to avoid being vulnerable at ground level.

Whenever you enter into a multi-story building, be sure to explore all the floors, including the basement and attic. You'll often find Chests and rare weapons in the more secluded or harder-to-reach areas of buildings or houses.

Check under staircases, as well as behind objects and furniture, to find weapons, along with Chests that contain the most useful loot (and weapons).

Walking through water is a slow process. It also leaves you out in the open and vulnerable to an attack.

To cross a wide river or lake quickly, simply build a flat bridge and walk across it.

If you have the time and extra resources, build a raised bridge to cross a river or lake. When time permits, destroy bridges after you cross them, or your adversaries might use them to follow your footsteps and hunt you down.

For added protection from sniper attacks, for example, consider building a covered bridge with walls and a ceiling.

The Weather Forecast is Awful: A Deadly Storm is Always Approaching

A deadly storm is looming from the moment you land on the island. Every few minutes, as the storm encompasses more of the island, this makes more and more of the land uninhabitable. In other words, if you get caught in the storm, your health diminishes and you'll eventually perish.

As larger portions of the island get engulfed by the storm, the negative impact of being caught in the storm steadily increases. Use the map to determine where the storm is and in what direction it's moving.

The storm forces all surviving heroes to continuously move into a smaller and smaller area as the battle progresses. Ideally, you want to stay in the safe areas of the island and avoid the storm altogether, but this isn't always possible. Just keep your time in the storm limited and use first-aid items to replenish your Health and Shields to survive longer.

© Epic Games, Inc.

Ideally, you want to stay near the center of the circle (the non-purple area of the map), where you're safe from the storm.

A common strategy is to stay near the edge of the storm (on the safe side), and position yourself with a long-range weapon so you can target and defeat enemies as they also move into the safe area after they themselves were caught in the storm. This typically works best as the circle of habitable land gets smaller, and more surviving heroes are forced into closer proximity.

If you get stuck on the deadly side of the storm and need to run forward to move into a still-clear area, cross the storm's threshold with your most powerful weapon drawn and ready to fire. There will likely be enemies waiting for you as you exit the storm. Chances are you'll be weak, due to damage to your Health and Shields caused by the storm.

When moving around inside the storm, not only will you get weaker and weaker the more time you spend there, but you'll also move slower. Follow the white or blue line on the map that's displayed in the top-right corner of the screen to find your way to clearer skies.

Spend too much time in the storm and you'll wind up eliminating yourself from the battle once your Health reaches 0HP. To extend the amount of time you can spend inside the deadly storm, before you enter into it, use Bandages, or drink Slurp Juice or a Chug Jug.

SECTION 4
FIND AND GATHER THE BEST WEAPONS, AMMO, AND LOOT

There are many types of weapons available on the island. Each weapon type is color-coded based on its rarity. The rarest weapons tend to be the most powerful, which typically determines how accurately it can be aimed, how quickly it can be reloaded, how much ammo is can hold, and how much damage a direct hit will cause. Orange weapons are the most rare. Epic Games adds new weapon types to the game on a pretty regular basis.

Each weapon category includes a selection of similar weapons you can find and use. The difference between types of weapons in the same category (such as Pistols) is the number of rounds of ammo each can hold, how quickly the weapon can be reloaded, and the type of ammo each uses.

The main categories of weapons you'll encounter include:

- **Assault Rifles:** Ideal for close or mid-range combat, these are powerful weapons that can cause serious damage when aimed correctly. Some Assault Rifles are equipped with a scope. This makes them ideal for long-range combat and sniping.
- **Explosives:** This weapon category includes hand grenades and RPGs that can be tossed or shot from a distance. The resulting explosion can instantly defeat enemies, plus damage or destroy structures. If you and an opponent are fighting from a distance, a Sniper Rifle will allow you to carefully aim and shoot an enemy, while an explosive weapon will damage or destroy everything that's close to where it lands.

© Epic Games, Inc.

A Rocket Launcher is a rare weapon. It's one of the Explosive weapons that comes in very handy if you manage to be one of the final few soldiers remaining on the island.

- **Hunting Rifle:** This is one of the newer weapons to be added to the game. It's a mid- to long-range weapon, with no scope required to achieve good aim. Only one round of ammo fits into the chamber at a time, so plan on taking time to reload between shots. This weapon is considered rare and can be found in Chests or on the floor in some buildings or structures.
- **Pistols:** These are the least powerful, and are only useful for close-range combat. If you need to free up space in your backpack for more powerful weapons, pistols should be the first weapon(s) you get rid of.

© Epic Games, Inc.

When you walk up to a weapon lying on the ground, a pop-up window will tell you what type of weapon it is. A Revolver, for example, is one type of Pistol that can be found in many areas of the island.

A basic Pistol is good for close-range combat and is common. However, it's one of the least powerful weapons available to you.

- **Shotguns:** These weapons don't hold a lot of ammo, so you'll need to reload often. This delays how long it takes to shoot multiple bullets at your target. Shotguns are better for close to mid-range combat. Be ready to reload quickly, or switch weapons when enemies are nearby. Consider hiding behind an object or structure while you're reloading so you're not out in the open and an easy target.

- **SMGs (Sub Machine Guns):** These are more powerful weapons than pistols and can hold much more ammo between reloads. They're harder to aim but cause more damage. They're also well suited to close- to mid-range combat.

- **Sniper Rifles:** As a long-range weapon, these are the most useful for accurately aiming and shooting enemies from a distance. Aim for a headshot whenever possible to inflict the most harm to a soldier. A highly skilled sniper, who shoots from high above their opponents while crouching behind an object or wall, is difficult to defeat.

When using an Assault Rifle or Burst Assault Rifle, for example, press the Aiming button on your controller to zoom in on your subject. This gives you much more accurate aiming capabilities from a distance. It takes a bit longer to target your weapon, but from a distance will allow you to achieve more devastating results.

Using a weapon with a scope really allows you to zoom in on your intended target from a distance, and it greatly improves your aiming accuracy.

Activating a Scope allows you to really zoom in on your enemy from far away. To improve your aim even further, crouch when you shoot.

© Epic Games, Inc.

You can walk, run, or tiptoe and shoot at the same time using almost any weapon, but doing this reduces your aiming accuracy, often dramatically. You will typically waste a lot of ammo trying to hit your target. When possible, stand absolutely still when shooting.

© Epic Games, Inc.

If you crouch when you aim your weapon, your accuracy improves. This also makes you a smaller target for your enemies.

Some weapons come with unlimited ammo. Others require you to find ammo and pick it up. There are also a handful of weapons that require you to craft ammo once you run out. In this situation, you'll need to have the right resources on hand.

Look carefully for green ammo boxes. They don't glow or make a sound, like Chests and weapons. What's inside will replenish your ammunition supply for weapons that need a refill.

Acquiring the Loot You'll Need

In order to custom-build structures you'll first need to acquire resources: wood, brick (stone), and metal. Using your Pickaxe, you can smash just about any object in the game, allowing you to gain resources from it.

Trees, most buildings, fences, and wooden crates are ideal sources of wood. Trees with the thickest trunks provide the most wood.

Rock formations and demolishing brick or stone walls are the best sources for stone, which get transformed into bricks for building.

Anything metal you destroy with your Pickaxe, such as cars, trucks, tractors (shown), buses, RVs, and metal fencing, as well as appliances found in a business or home, can be used to build structures and objects out of metal.

Metal furniture or appliances are a great source for metal.

© Epic Games, Inc.

Anytime you use the Pickaxe on an abandoned vehicle, its horn will often honk and make a lot of noise. While a vehicle will generate a lot of metal, it'll also attract a lot of attention, and you could easily reveal your location.

© Epic Games, Inc.

To speed up the wood, brick, and metal resource collection process, aim your Pickaxe at the circular targets that appear on the object you're chopping at. If you hit the same target twice quickly, this increases the amount of resources you receive from that object.

Continuously displayed on the screen is the amount of wood, brick, and metal you've collected. In order to custom-build anything, such as walls, floors, ceilings, pyramid-shaped roofs, stairs, doors, or ramps, you will need to have an ample supply of resources at your disposal.

As you're exploring, look for resource icons (for wood, brick, and metal) lying on the ground. These icons can also be found in some Chests. When you grab one, it provides a bonus supply of that resource without your having to use your Pickaxe.

Once you enter into building mode, select what you want to build, then choose which resource you want to build with. Anything you build is easily visible to all enemies nearby. So if you're building a structure for protection, use the strongest material at your disposal. Depending on how quickly you need protection, it's sometimes better to seek cover from a pre-constructed building, structure, or nearby object as opposed to building your own.

Need a bird's eye view of the terrain around you? Build a tall ramp like this one, and climb to the top. Just don't accidently fall off the ramp's edge, or you probably won't survive the fall. At the very least, the level of your Health HP meter will take a hit.

Check out the stunning view from the top of this tall ramp over-looking Greasy Grove. Using a long-range sniper rifle, for example, you can hit enemies below you from this vantage point.

Grab Whatever Supplies (Loot) You Can Find

In addition to weapons and ammo, scattered throughout the island (often in houses and buildings) and in Chests and supply drops are other useful items, including:

- **Bandages:** Each time you use one Bandage, it replenish 15HP (Health Points), out of a possible 100. The good news is that you can use up to five Bandages in a row, if you have them in your inventory. Each Bandage takes a few seconds to apply, so make sure you're in a safe place when you use them. Avoid becoming a vulnerable target.

© Epic Games, Inc.

Bandages are often found in Chests, but sometimes you'll see them lying around inside pre-existing buildings or houses, for example.

- **Campfire:** This is one of the newest items to be added to the game. Once you light a campfire, for every second you stand close to it, your Health HP increases by one unit. Thus, if you enjoy the warmth of the fire for a full minute or so, your Health meter will fully replenish. Only use a campfire in locations that are well protected, because you'll be vulnerable to attack. Consider building a wall around it before you light it. Once lit, a campfire will attract attention from enemies nearby. If you have teammates, they too can stand close to the same campfire and benefit from its healing capabilities.

- **Chug Jug:** One drink and you'll restore your full Health and Shields. The drawback is that each drink takes 15 seconds to consume, during which time you can't do anything else, so make sure you're well protected while drinking.

- **Jetpacks:** This is another item that was more recently added to the game as a way for soldiers to reach new heights without having to construct ramps or stairs.

- **Med Kits:** Immediately restore full Health to your soldier. You're able to carry up to three Med Kits in one slot of your backpack's inventory.

- **Shield Potions:** Keep these in your backpack, and take a quick drink when your Shield meter is running low. There are Regular Shield Potions, which give you 50 extra Shield HP points, and Small Shield Potions, which give you 25 extra Shield HP points.

Blue Shield Potions are the most powerful, and can usually be found in Chests. Drinking a Blue Shield Potion will give you a 50HP increase in Shield capabilities for the duration of the battle. As soon as you find one, drink it!

- **Slurp Juice:** Restores 25 Health and 25 Shield HP points. Use in conjunction with Bandages to restore your Health to 100HP.

Grab Slurp Juice when you come across it, and take a drink when you need a Health and Shield boost. While you're drinking, you become vulnerable to attack, so make sure you're in a secure location, surrounded by walls, for example.

- **Traps:** Once you find Traps, you can carry them around and place them within structures. A well-placed Trap on a wall, floor, or ceiling will instantly and passively defeat an enemy without you having to be nearby. Meanwhile, Traps can also be used against you, so any time you enter a structure or building built by someone else, for example, proceed with caution.

© Epic Games, Inc.

If you have Traps at your disposal, consider building a small square structure with a doorway. Place the Trap so it's unseen inside the door, leave the structure, and close the door behind you. Consider leaving a powerful weapon or item from your backpack outside of the door as a lure to attract enemies inside.

© Epic Games, Inc.

Once you've collected a Trap, select it while in building mode and choose exactly where you want to place it.

© Epic Games, Inc.

After setting a trap, don't move in too close to it, or you'll set it off yourself and wind up leaving the battle in disgrace.

© Epic Games, Inc.

In your Inventory, you can only hold five gear items at a time. A gear item is something that you need to manually pick up (such as a weapon, potion, or Bandages). If your backpack is full and you discover a new and super-powerful weapon, to grab it you'll first need to give up one item in your backpack, so choose whatever is least important to your survival.

If you need to free up space in your backpack, instead of leaving unused Potions or Bandages behind if your Health or Shield meter are not at 100 percent, choose from the items, then grab whatever newly found item or weapon you think will be more useful to you.

When you need healing but have no potions handy, find a safe place to hide, then give yourself a chance to regain some of your strength by resting.

© Epic Games, Inc.

Look, up in the sky! If you see a small hot air balloon with a Chest attached to it, it's a Supply Drop. The Chest is chock full of useful goodies, including weapons and other items. Wait for it to land, and approach it with caution.

© Epic Games, Inc.

The trick with Supply Drops is being the first person to reach it once it lands. Approach with caution! If enemies are nearby, they might also try to get what's inside the Supply Drop, or hide nearby, wait for you to be out in the open gathering the loot, and launch a surprise attack.

© Epic Games, Inc.

Just like when you open a Chest, a Supply Drop will scatter the items in it on the ground around you. Pick and choose what you want to grab. Focus on the rare and more powerful weapons, for example.

SECTION 5
BUILD FORTRESSES & STRUCTURES LIKE A PRO

Building is an important component to Fortnite: Battle Royale. After entering into building mode, your character can use resources you've collected to build a wall, ceiling, floor, pyramid-shaped roof, or ramp/stairs, using different shaped tiles.

A single Wall tile is about to be constructed here.

Use this option to place a ceiling or floor tile. Once you select this option, position the cursor upwards or downwards, based on where you want to build.

A pyramid-shaped roof tile can be used as a ceiling for a structure, or placed on the floor to serve as a protective shield that your soldier can hide behind.

Using stair/ramp tiles alone allows you to quickly build a way for you to reach higher levels. Choose wood to build most of your ramps, and save your stone and metal for structures that you'll need to protect yourself behind.

© Epic Games, Inc.

Stairs made out of stone (brick) take longer to build.

© Epic Games, Inc.

Ultimately, you'll combine using different-shaped tiles to create simple or elaborate structures. Use your own creativity to come up with building designs, or study the work of more experienced Fortnite players.

In addition to creating and placing one tile at a time, such as a wall or ramp, use Turbo Building to quickly build and place multiple tiles in quick succession. To do this, choose a type of building tile and a building material, then press and hold down the building button on your controller or keyboard. You'll be able to keep building and placing the pieces quickly until you run out of resources.

There will be times when you approach a structure you can't easily get to. The solution is to take a few steps back and build a ramp from wood.

Select the Ramp building option, then choose wood. Use the Turbo Building feature to build and walk or run up the ramp at the same time.

In no time, you'll have easy access to whatever it was you could not previously reach without building.

The key to becoming an expert builder is practice! Learn how to build the structures you need quickly, then grab a weapon from your inventory so you can defend yourself or launch an attack from the structure you've built.

As soon as a battle begins, your first priority should be to get your hands on one or more weapons with ammo. Only then should you start collecting resources to build with.

From the Game menu, turn on Auto Material Change. When it's active, as you're Turbo Building, if you run out of the material you were using, you'll immediately and automatically switch to another resource you already have on hand. This is a great timesaver. The Turbo Building feature also needs to be turned on from the Game menu. Access Settings, select the Game menu, then scroll down to turn on Auto Material Change and Turbo Building options.

Especially in the early stages of a battle, you don't need to build a fully enclosed structure to protect yourself. Sometimes just a ramp, pyramid-shaped roof piece, or just a single wall will be adequate. Don't waste building resources unless you need to.

© Epic Games, Inc.

Using Turbo Building is particularly useful when building a bridge, a long or tall ramp, or a cube-shaped structure around yourself. When creating a pathway or ramp, build and move at the same time.

If you're exposed and vulnerable to an enemy attack, quickly build a wall in front of you to use as a shield. If you don't know the direction from which an attack might come, build a box (four walls) or a cube (four walls with a floor and ceiling) around yourself.

Especially when using Turbo Build mode, it's much quicker to build with wood than with stone (bricks) or metal. Then, while one of your structures is being shot at, you can use resources (if you have them) to conduct repairs.

© Epic Games, Inc.

Assuming you're skilled enough to survive until the late stages of a battle, when only a few enemies remain and the amount of inhabitable land on the island is very small, be sure you stock up on all resources—wood, brick, and metal—so you can build a strong and very tall fortress. From the fortress, use a sniper rifle or RPG, for example, to shoot and hopefully defeat the remaining enemies. In most situations, avoid being on or near ground level when only a few enemies remain.

If you think a nearby enemy has a grenade launcher or another projectile weapon, build a ceiling onto a structure you're hiding in to prevent a grenade from landing directly on your head.

Especially in the late stages of a battle, make sure you have at least 300 to 500 units of stone or metal on hand to rebuild fortresses that take damage. If you can't rebuild or repair your fortress, which will typically be your last safe stronghold, you become extremely vulnerable to enemy attacks. If your fort gets too damaged, built a bridge to a nearby treetop and hide there. Use a sniper rifle or RPG, for example, to attack enemies, but keep in mind, as soon as you fire an explosive weapon, your location will be revealed.

Remember, any time you're exploring a house, you're more apt to find a Chest in the attic than on a main level. To reach an attic, however, you'll often need to build stairs or a ramp. If you smash through a ceiling above you with your Pickaxe, and the Chest winds up falling through the floor, everything in it will be lost.

How to Create a Window and Door in a Wall

When hiding in a structure you've built or behind a wall you've constructed to serve as a shield, you have the option of editing the wall and adding a window or door.

Once you've mastered the skills required to quickly build, invest time learning how to edit walls quickly so you can easily add windows or doors to most of your structures.

To create a window in a structure you've built, follow these steps:

Step #1: First build a solid wall.

Step #2: Face the wall and press the appropriate button to enter into Edit mode. Move the cursor to the box where you want to create the window.

© Epic Games, Inc.

Step #3: Press the Confirm button to proceed. The window will be created.

© Epic Games, Inc.

It's also possible to build a door into a wall you've already built. To do this, face the wall and enter into Edit mode. Use the cursor to select one box.

© Epic Games, Inc.

Move the cursor to a second box (above or below the first one), and select it as well.

© Epic Games, Inc.

With two boxes (one on top of the other) on the wall selected, press the Confirm button to build the door. Once it's built, you can open and close it just like any other door, using the Open button on your controller or keyboard.

Traps that you've collected during your exploration can be placed on a floor, ceiling, or wall within a structure. The building menu on the game screen will add a Trap option once you've collected at least one Trap.

When you're ready to use a Trap, select it from the Build menu, and direct the cursor to place it where you want to set it. Press the Confirm button to set the Trap. Now, make sure you don't accidently set it off yourself!

© Epic Games, Inc.

Keep in mind that you can often build your own structures inside preexisting structures, such as houses or buildings, and you can build just about anywhere outside. It's possible to build a bridge between two buildings so you can stay high up, or to build on top of a pre-existing building so you can get yourself even higher up.

Ultimately, the key to becoming a master builder is speed. But to be able to build fast and sturdy structures, be sure to practice collecting resources and building different types of structures in various types of terrain. Since there's no tutorial mode included in Battle Royale, to practice building, jump off of the Battle Bus in a secluded area. This way, your chance of encountering enemies is significantly lower.

Structures You Build Can Be Repaired

Don't forget, if a structure you've built gets damaged, as long as you have enough resources available, you can repair it during or after an incoming attack.

© Epic Games, Inc.

Damaged structures begin to appear transparent before they're destroyed entirely. To start a repair, face the damaged wall or area and activate Edit mode. Select the Repair option, and choose the resource you'd like to use. Place the cursor over the damaged tiles to determine what areas need repair, and tap the Confirm button. Learning to initiate repairs quickly during an attack will keep you alive longer.

When your structure is under attack by nonexplosive weapons, consider building upwards, so you can get up higher than your enemy to launch a counterattack. Should you see or hear a grenade or RPG coming at you, consider evacuating the structure and temporarily seeking cover elsewhere.

© Epic Games, Inc.

If you see your walls becoming transparent during a battle, initiate repairs, build more walls, or retreat, depending on the situation. Whatever you do, make a decision and react quickly, or you're a goner.

© Epic Games, Inc.

Instead of repairing a wall or roof tile, you can always double-up and add a second layer of protection. If there's room, leave a little space between the two layers of walls to put extra distance between you and the attacker. Shown here is a wood wall, along with a brick ramp, plus a brick wall, which a soldier can stand behind for a triple layer of protection.

SECTION 6

SURVIVING COMBAT TO BECOME THE LAST PERSON STANDING

The moment you spot an enemy nearby, your first instinct might be to fire your weapon(s) to defeat that opponent. Sometimes this is worthwhile, but consider your current circumstances.

Especially early in the battle, if you're able to safely hide and go unnoticed, you may be better off allowing the enemy to go off and continue doing whatever it is he was doing. Each time you confront an enemy, one of several things could happen that you need to consider:

- You could discover he's better armed than you, and lose the fight.
- If the enemy recently consumed a potion, his Health and Shields could be maxed out, making him much harder to defeat.
- The adversary may be luring you into a Trap.
- If he's skilled at building, he might quickly construct a protective barrier before he launches his own attack against you to defend himself.
- Other enemies could be lurking nearby and the noise from your battle could alert them of your presence.

Remember, when you fire your weapon(s), you make noise that can be heard by everyone else nearby. Even if you're able to defeat the first enemy you see, you could easily attract unwanted attention and quickly find yourself outgunned and overpowered by several other adversaries at once.

An RPG can literally blow the roof off a structure and defeat whomever is inside. Here, only three soldiers remain in the battle, so staying stealthy is not as important as using your most powerful weapon to defeat the remaining adversaries from the greatest distance possible.

Some projectile weapons, including RPGs, have a very visible tracer once they're fired, so others can quickly determine from where the weapon was launched. This could easily give away your position, leaving you vulnerable to attack.

Anytime you manage to kill an enemy, especially later on in battles, do not immediately run up to collect the loot they've left behind. Chances are other nearby enemies heard your fight and are watching from a distance. They could be hiding and waiting to launch an attack with a sniper rifle, for example.

Make sure the path to your fallen enemy is clear. Once you reach the defeated enemy, consider quickly building a box around you and the loot, so you're protected as you decide what loot to take and what, if anything, needs to be left behind. This also applies to collecting loot from Supply Drops or Chests.

If your backpack is already full, but you discover a potion or drink that you need to consume, make sure you're safe, drop the weapon you're holding, grab and drink the portion or drink, and re-grab the weapon. You'll be temporarily vulnerable to attack while drinking, but can partially or entirely replenish your Health and/or Shields.

Early on in a battle, don't waste time and resources building an elaborate and strong fortress. Stick with basic ramps and structures unless you need more elaborate defenses to protect against an incoming attack. Save the resources until only a few enemies remain and you're confined to a small area of the map. This is when building a tall and strong fortress (like the one shown here made of brick) becomes essential.

© Epic Games, Inc.

Running low on weapons, potions, and other loot is a huge mistake. Since Chests are always located in the same place, memorize their locations in each area so you can stock up when needed (as long as someone else hasn't emptied the Chest before you). In this case, the soldier who first opened the Chest probably needed to leave some items behind. At the very least, grab their leftovers.

Once you're defeated, don't immediately exit the battle and return to the Lobby. Instead, stay in Spectating mode, and study the fighting and building strategies used by the remaining heroes. The last players standing tend to be the pros, and you can learn a lot by watching them in action. Plus, you can get ideas about how to construct fortresses and structures in future battles.

© Epic Games, Inc.

Here, there are four soldiers remaining, the storm is closing in, and a Supply Drop has just fallen in the distance. This soldier is hiding behind a tree waiting to shoot at whoever approaches the Supply Drop. Sometimes, collecting what's offered by a Supply Drop is not worth the risk, unless you're desperate for supplies.

© Epic Games, Inc.

Of course, another way to replenish supplies is to defeat an opponent and collect what they've left behind. Here, the player built and hid behind a wooden wall for protection while he evaluated the loot available to him after a successful gun fight.

© Epic Games, Inc.

© Epic Games, Inc.

Use pre-created structures and your surroundings to your advantage. If you're already in an enclosed or tight space, such as when exploring the Shifty Shafts mines, keep your back to the wall and your weapon targeted at the openings or doorways an enemy might approach from. If you crouch and tiptoe, you won't make noise, so you can catch an enemy by surprise while they're exploring too.

This also applies if you're in a small room with just one door. Just make sure a sniper can't shoot you through a window you're not paying attention to. (Don't stand in front of windows.) If necessary, build a wall to cover the window in a pre-existing structure so you can focus on guarding the door.

As you jump from the Battle Bus, it's often useful to land on a roof and smash your way down into the attic. In this house (found near Greasy Grove), for example, you'll discover a nicely equipped Chest in the attic, as well as plenty of other weapons and loot in the main areas of the house.

SECTION 7

YOUR TRAINING HAS ONLY JUST BEGUN: FORTNITE RESOURCES

Progamers around the world have created YouTube channels, online forums, and blogs focused exclusively on Fortnite: Battle Royale. Plus, you can watch pro players compete online and describe their best strategies, or check out the coverage of Fortnite: Battle Royale published by leading gaming websites and magazines.

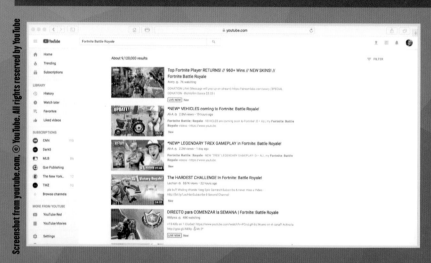

On YouTube (www.youtube.com), YouTube Gaming (https://gaming.youtube.com), or Twitch.TV (https://www.twitch.tv/directory/game/Fortnite), in the Search field, enter the search phrase "Fortnite Battle Royale" to discover many game-related channels and videos. (YouTube.com is shown here.)

Be sure to check out these awesome online resources that will help you become a better Fortnite: Battle Royale player:

WEBSITE OR YOUTUBE CHANNEL NAME	DESCRIPTION	URL
Epic Games's Fortnite YouTube Channel	The official Fortnight YouTube channel.	www.youtube.com/user/epicfortnite
Epic Games's official Fortnite website	Learn all about Fortnite: Battle Royale, as well as the paid editions of Fortnite.	www.epicgames.com/fortnite
Epic Games's official Twitter feed for Fortnite	The official Fortnite Twitter feed.	https://twitter.com/fortnitegame (@fortnitegame)
Fandom's Fortnite Wiki	Discover the latest news and strategies related to Fortnite.	http://fortnite.wikia.com/wiki/Fortnite_Wiki
FBR Insider	The Fortnite: Battle Royale Insider website offers game-related news, tips, and strategy videos.	www.fortniteinsider.com
IGN Entertainment's Fortnite Coverage	Check out all IGN's past and current coverage of Fortnite.	www.ign.com/wikis/fortnite
Microsoft's Xbox One Fortnite Website	Learn about and acquire Fortnite: Battle Royale if you're an Xbox One gamer.	www.microsoft.com/en-US/store/p/Fortnite-Battle-Royalee/BT5P2X999VH2
Nomxs	A YouTube channel hosted by online personality Simon Britton (Nomxs). It features Fortnite game streams.	https://youtu.be/np-8cmsUZmc
Rhinocrunch's "How NOT to be a Noob (Fortnite: Battle Royale)"	This strategy-intensive YouTube video is a "must see" if you're serious about improving your gameplay skills.	https://youtu.be/uMgtS5MSuOA

(Continued on next page)

Skill Up's "Fortnite: Battle Royale – Top 10 Beginner's Tips)"	A useful YouTube video for learning Fornite basics.	https://youtu.be/ DuwCBPl_FQk
Sony's PS4 Fortnite Website	Learn about and acquire Fortnite if you're a PS4 gamer.	www.playstation.com/en-us/ games/fortnite-ps4
ThatDenverGuy's "9 Common Mistakes New Players Make – Fortnite: Battle Royale Tips and Tricks"	This YouTube video explains how to avoid common mistakes Fortnite players make.	https://youtu.be/ Z0zBx0vdARE
The Gamer Couple's "50 Advanced Tips to Become a God in Fortnite"	Learn awesome tips to improve your skills when playing Fortnite from this information-packed YouTube video.	https://youtu.be/ ONS-Bz-k1-Q

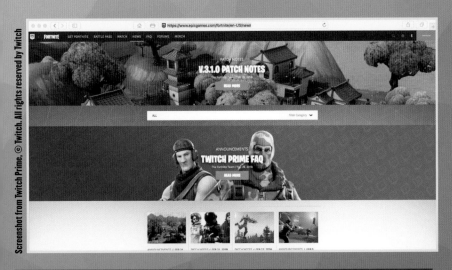

Point your web browser to Epic Games's Fortnite News page (www.epic-games.com/fortnite/en-US/news) to discover what new features have just been added to Fortnite: Battle Royale, plus get a preview of what's on the way.

IGN.com offers extensive news and tip-oriented coverage of Fortnite.

Unless your TV or monitor has excellent speakers, consider using good-quality headphones to hear the sound while playing Fortnite.

FINAL THOUGHTS

In just a few short months, Fortnite: Battle Royale has become one of the most popular computer and video games in the world. Thanks to recent (or pending) updates, it's now possible to play online - against 99 other people - whether those other gamers are experiencing Fortnite on a PC, Mac, PS4, Xbox One, iPhone, iPad, or Android-based mobile device.

Along with the ever-changing challenges you'll encounter from your opponents in each battle, Epic Games is doing an incredible job at continuously updating, adding to, and tweaking the game to make it more exciting and challenging for gamers at all skill levels.

For example, on March 15, 2018, a new type of weapon, called Remote Explosives, was introduced. If you collect one of these weapons, place it on an enemy structure and then run away. When your enemy enters the structure, remotely detonate the explosive, and it'll instantly demolish the structure and potentially eliminate your enemy with a single boom.

From reading this book, now that you've learned a collection of strategies and tips that can help you be victorious, the next thing you want to do is keep practicing. Only one person will end each battle alive and victorious, but even if you're constantly getting defeated, you can have an awesome time playing Fortnite: Battle Royale as you continuously strive to improve your fighting, shooting, building, and exploration strategies.

Stay focused. Keep practicing. Don't give up, and most importantly, HAVE FUN!